Black Crow Dress

ROXANE BETH JOHNSON

ALICE JAMES BOOKS
FARMINGTON, MAINE

10 9 8 7 6 5 4 3 2 1

Alice James Books are published by Alice James Poetry Cooperative, Inc.,
an affiliate of the University of Maine at Farmington.

Alice James Books
238 Main Street
Farmington, ME 04938
www.alicejamesbooks.org

Library of Congress Cataloging-in-Publication Data

Johnson, Roxane Beth.
   Black crow dress / Roxane Beth Johnson.
      p. cm.
   Includes bibliographical references and index.
   ISBN 978-1-882295-95-1 (pbk.)
   I. Title.
   PS3610.O3755B57 2013
   811'.6--dc23

                              2012029617

Alice James Books gratefully acknowledges support from individual donors, private foundations,
the University of Maine at Farmington, and the National Endowment for the Arts.

ART WORKS.
arts.gov

Cover Art:
Betye Saar (b.1926)
Black Girl's Window, 1969
mixed-media assemblage
35 3/4" x 18" x 1 1/2"
Credit Line: Collection of the artist; Courtesy of Michael Rosenfeld Gallery LLC, New York, NY

Contents

i.

ii.

...
iii.

Acknowledgments

Grateful acknowledgment is due to the editors of the following literary magazines and online publications where these poems (or altered versions of them) have appeared:

The Georgia Review: "Plenty" (published as "Emancipation")

Beloit Poetry Journal: "Prudence Finch Remembers Her Slave, Clea: Second Memory" (published as "Prudence Finch Remembers Her Slave, Clea")

Calalloo: "How This Book Begins: I Wake to a Roomful of Slaves" (published as "I Wake to a Roomful of Slaves")

Reed Magazine: "Slave Ancestors Found Unburied in a Dream"

Zoland Poetry Review: "Clea's Workday"(published as "Clea. House Slave. Work Day."), and "Zebedee States the Reason for His Visit" (published as "A Slave Ancestor States the Reason for His Visit"), and "Dream Visitor"

Sentence: A Journal of Prose Poetics: "Hush-Harbor Scene: The Slaves Sing" (published as "Hush-Harbor Scene") and "Middle Passage"

An Introduction to the Prose Poem: "Middle Passage"

Black Arts Quarterly: "Tobias Finch Tells How He Raped His 11-Year-Old Slave, Clea;" "Clea's Side of the Story;" "To Auction;" "Escape with Shirt and Body;" and "Dream Visitor"

Common-Place: "Caroline Remembers Her First Mistress, Darla Ford," "Zebedee Tells What It's Like to Be Sold" (published as "Zebedee Ponders What It's Like to be Sold"), and "Clea, Living and Dying" (published as "Living and Dying: Clea's Reincarnation")

Connotation Press: An Online Artifact: "Clea's Ghost Comes for an Extended Visit" (published as "The Poet's Notes: Clea Comes for an Extended Visit), "Prudence Finch's Dream about Clea" (published as "Prudence Finch Sits in My Kitchen and Tells Clea about a Dream She Had Many Years After Emancipation"), "The Slaves Arrive and Do Not Leave for Months," "Zebedee Walking Behind Slave Quarters at Night" (published as "Zebedee the Mulatto Walking Behind Slave Quarters at Night"), and "Prudence Finch Remembers Her Slave, Clea: First Memory"

To my sister, Rebekah

i.

Slave Ancestors Found Unburied in a Dream

Each one is hungry for a voice and music to re-bloom
them alive in this room like water softens beans.
Leaning near, close to me they see my tooth and tongue
that test doneness, licks stamps and hums.
Their ear listens to what a hand might fiddle
if it had fingers.
Stare this way with eyes like smudges, give me scars
to mark dreaming at the place it fades out to.
How the heart in living that was bound to flesh
of self and another does skip and quiver, play replay
the syllable it gets stuck on. Hungry is, but can live
on silvery skin scraped from salmon, the dish of milk
the cat lets yellow.
Gone is shame, left behind with name and dates.
Dance to music reckless as dogs that chased them
up trees, aching for a throat.
Shimmy out of skin, let it wind down
to a rind at my feet.

How This Book Begins:
I Wake to a Roomful of Slaves

They whir up like a jukebox, sing of time telling all, then fill my lungs with mud. I pray their teeth in my throat will loosen. Soft hands furiously pull up wheat. Bodies bent and they limp; no rest though dead. I give them bread to eat; they rub their bellies and ask for a cup of leaves. Their mouths full of poverty, they drink my sleep. What more do they want? This life to flower, this world to unfold, some ground, some fire and a bowl of seed. They want what never was. I am their one warm bed. I am the only land they will ever own.

Middle Passage

Don't give me no words on a page to describe my sufferings.
Don't tell me you can speak the stench rising up thick as flies.
I'll tell you my eyes burned with piss and the sun lit on nothing
but the bleeding wounds on my back. Don't worry about me
now, packed tight in that slop jar, holding the slippery hip of
some woman not mine. I got no lessons from the dying, no
peace from the spirits I begged to help us. I tell you none of
them came, though I always gave them meat. Don't look at me
with your pity. I don't cry no tears. Ever. The taste just reminds
me of the sea.

Tobias Finch Discusses His Obsession from the Grave: His Slave, Caroline

I own one hundred slaves. Bought my fair Caroline last. Queen of my bee-stung heart. Something so of the walnut about her. A fortune of meat crowded in her. Some tenderness I want to crack open like a storm. Her shaky lips are wet. I touch them. That strumpet. She is nothing but my absolute. She festoons me like a blister.

Tobias Finch Discusses His Two Children: Prudence and the Mulatto Zebedee

This child of mine and Caroline was born white as I, that Zebedee. My wife tried to kill him. Fool she ever was. Meanwhile, my girl Prudence plucked at my heart to the hairs on my head. She'd often touch a nigger's hand serving soup. Idiot. That child had a mind that grew thorns in my soul. That beast I had with Caroline shared my blood and I feared it. Shared something I ought not have given. And Prudence emerged from my wish for a proper son by being born a girl. To the end, Prudence will bang me like a drum. That boy could call me father. My children eat me like moths.

Prudence Finch Remembers Her Slave, Clea: First Memory

Daddy bought me one, a girl. I was seven and she was five. She had hands black as velvet and fingernails the color of skinned peaches.

She was a full moon, light's bright fist. She reminded me of strange birds I saw in picture books: a toucan or a raven.

She was sluggish as turtles in baskets that the cook would make into soup. She wouldn't do what I told her. She sat in the shade, nested in her silence. Her quiet was a boat.

Her open palms were pink roses that held her albatrosses. They roosted near ponds, grew wingless and sat on eggs that never hatched.

The Slaves Tell about Mistress Finch

Consider the mistress who stopped feeding her oldest slave. See that old one she refused scraps and bread. See his hands holding his own flesh, his face an apple bruise. Hear her tell the others, *Feed him and I'll whip you 'till you bleed.* See he is not surprised by this latest misconduct. I ask you, what about this mistress who stopped feeding this old slave? Watch her read the leather book, ponder the mother asking for John's head on a platter. See her mind frying in its own fat. Her body filling with stones. But back to this dying slave: do you see him wandering like a broken-down horse, eating cobwebs and grass? Do you spy the mistress watching from her window? Did you catch that fly, how it keeps going in and out of his mouth? Listen to her compare a slave to a goat and turn away from the evening's meat. You know, they'll both die bad as rabbits torn by crows. You know they both prayed to God. Do you know whose story it is we should tell?

Seven Years Later Prudence Finch Cared for Her Half Brother, Zebedee

Father chained Zebedee in the barn at night. He could run off and because he was so white no one would stop him. In the horse house Father put him where his bed was straw and coal. I was seven years, one year older than him. I worried about flares of cold; his feet were pink covering bones frail as fish. I held my own and considered: could they snap? I knew things my parents didn't. I saw wide as a barn owl. I brought him a blanket. Simple as that. Two potatoes for his feet to warm, but he ate them when I turned my back. I learned to lean on sleep and not fall through its tempting door. I rose with the birds, the sky they filled like lungs with smoky air. I got the blanket, ran home—I was so fast I was blurry as blinking. If father caught me my body would be his machinery tightened up to screaming then sprung like a watch. The air at night was full of ash. Horses shifted. Zebedee wondered me. The barn was full of eyes.

The Slaves Tell All

Zebedee was born so white the mistress took him to the meat
block to kill him. Up to the hilt she was in spirits screaming.
She would be sprayed in blood soon. Her ears would ring with
singing. She'd extinguish her knife in his neck. She'd leave the
severed thing to breathe his last in the bright morning dark.
She'd walk off exquisite, pushing away the sound of those
wet mouths howling. *Damn slaves*, she'd holler. She'd wobble
shadows.

Fog brightened the sky. A hawk hovered. Her mind nudged
another way. Some say, *She wouldn't want some bird knowing her mind.*
Some say, *An old slave conjured her quick.* Some say, *Her mind slipped
down her throat.* Some say, *A noose got hold of her heart, squinched it tight.*

Did she throw the knife down? Maybe she let it slip. The knife
is still there; now it is a thorny thicket. Some say, *No one took the
baby.* Some say, *Zebedee is still there now, his breathing the sound of water
and hooves.* Each one say, *All our cryin' to keep his life just left him life
the mistress could sever with a gesture.* Some say, *There can't be no god
who'd let it all happen.* Some say, *Well now, even God let the white man
crucify His son.*

9

Caroline Remembers Her First Mistress, Darla Ford

When I think on it, it is of joy I recall. And knowing not. Not yet. *Ain't I got a pretty little crop of niggers coming on? Do my little niggers want some bread to gnaw on?* Small being what it was, our minds were full of maybes and the bread was good. White folk talk. Black folk quiet. Green leaves turn to gold then back to dirt like most things done gone by. Once the missus sliced my palm. She said, *Just to make sure your blood was red.* She cut and cut a line then dulled the embers snaking, now held my hand in mud. I could say things changed, everything was dark after that, after knowing she would cut me like a calf. I grew inward like a nail.

Prudence Finch Remembers Her Slave, Clea: Second Memory

Her hands on my piano are dark feathers dusting bones. She does not need music to play it.

Inside my head I keep true boxes clean (calendar days) and push what is pitiful to the black outlines (mother and father).

In my slave's heart are secret rooms and furniture I have not seen. She sits on a chair in herself and watches. Red at birth and red at death is the color, but what in between?

I want to know what she thinks of me, her secret scenery of opinion. I keep myself like a clock. She knows music like a mother, how to lean against it and learn its smell.

I am poor in myself, strange tree without fruit the Lord withers.

My slave is a spoon of honey. Mother's eyes scald milk and sharpen knives. I am whipped for saying she's sweet.

These are the bones of elephants, I tell my slave. *Tusks*, she says.

She breaks glasses and plates, and buries them. I like dirt's ability to hold what we wreck.

Tobias Finch Tells How He Raped His 11-Year-Old Slave, Clea

That girl lived in herself quiet as an instrument keeps music.
How bold her stillness, her ability to remain righteous as a torn
daisy no matter how I grabbed at her roots. I meant to unravel
her justice, find her private place. Learn her. A slave to study.
But, she was a green fruit in my mouth. A spiteful thing. How
daring her silence, as if she could hide. Who could have guessed
she would not flinch or beg, her eyes a trained voice, moving
about like a calf. The nimble slide of her neck. Her hands small
and crooked as walnut shells. How she seemed like my own
child. How outrageous that she would remind me. Her naked
figure nothing to me but a black stain on my clean, white sheet.

Clea's Side of the Story

Lord says make me an altar. My body is of a temple. Sweat cools on my skin like daylight on a wall it ebbs. Work then rest. Everyone in the fields all day. Doubt like Thomas it all continues yet occurring. Amen, amen. An orange is a world of sweetness sliced. I am a hidden clearing for dancing, spirit is a dove through trees flying. Sometimes I lay the seed, other times I stalk the birds. I am burned leaves crumbling in fire of red it rushes. Amen, amen. Lord says, don't be afraid of the body killed by hand but watch the price of your soul. At night, I have no mind left to dream. There is no treasure place to hide but the body. Lord says make an altar. I tried once with twigs. Everything is yet gone or stolen. I memorize a flight of crows. Let me think of folded hands. My body is of a temple. I put this there.

What Caroline Would Like to Say to Tobias Finch

Every bone in me belongs to you. I keep my soul and this color of singing. I keep the wet ground where seeds are born like my Jesus in a barn. Close my eyes and shake your touch like the prayerful ones in a clearing. I dream of angels climbing to heaven on gold ladders with the sound of hammers ringing. I remember rivers running black like ribbon. I keep all that. I keep my soul. You keep my bones and my body. You number every piece of me and jangle me like coins. You cut the threads that bind me and wonder why I flounder. I dream my face pressed to wood where Jesus' blood runs down like a blue stream. I keep my Lord's slow beating heart, slow as water come from a well. Every bone in His body rose up in the yellow morning light. You can go ahead and keep every bone in my body. All that mortality will stay buried in the ground. But, when I die, my soul you never did own will rise from ground like water turned into wine.

The Slaves Tell How Clea, Age 14, Is Ruined

It happened once that Clea ran away from the white man's naked hands, and the slave-catching dogs ate her. Imagine she died, see her soul leaving her body in many directions, leaves blown from a tree. Think of this tree, of planting beans out back or racking beneath the large maples. Leaves flowing and scattering. Sparrows and chickadees gripping the clean twigs, the milk white sky in between nubby branches. Imagine a few days later you get word that Clea lived. The dogs had torn her body in many places. She had no more breasts, but only one finger gone. Caroline sewed her with special thread and a needle made clean with fire. Massa and Misses said, *We don't know how she lived* and rubbed their hands like flies. It happened that we began to hear her breathing. Breath lavish as wind in summer trees, blowing the scent of prey, flowing over open wounds like salt.

Clea and Caroline Sing
a Workday Song

The Lord come to us in the cool of the day. In the cool of the day the Lord come. *Watch the moon,* He said, *watch it fill and watch it go.* How the night does fade. How this life will go. Go like a crow calling, taken like a lamb to the block. Don't fight the man who pulls you by the nose into the barn to slit your throat. Don't hold your own blood, girl, just let it go.

Hush-Harbor Scene: The Slaves Sing

When the crops were laid by, we went down to the water to have a little church. *Praise the spirit in holiness and be sanctified!* In a clearing, dust was quiet for dancing, our feet softly circled the earth. We sang steady as a cloud releasing its rain. Not a soul but ours knew how far we were into the night. *It is good and right always to praise His Name.* On Sunday, we wore some white; there was a baptism or two. Our cotton sacks and bonnets shimmied in the chilly night as the few went out to the lake's deep place where our sins were washed away. See the faces rising up from the water, slick as trout and wet with salvation. All day, we'd praise the Lord, thinking our souls are thick white flowers, blooming wide from rough dark branches.

How the Handsome Mulatto Zebedee, Age 18, Fell in Love with the Crippled Clea

She was good as a handful of silver money anyway. She made good ices. She licked my neck. She could play that piano without a first finger. How did she do that? She listened to my plans and kept them all in the nest of her hands. There she tended them with tiny twigs and bluebird eggs. She sat still as prayer, the thankful kind you pray when your belly is full. Quiet as grass. So rare. She was a fistful of seed.

ii.

Clea's First Note Sent to Zebedee

Everything open I leave—an omen for you. I leave the breadbox open, a glass empty and my shoes, with their leather mouths bent with no song. You, pass by my shoes and fill them with your looking. The kitchen window I crack, stick my fingers out and wave to you. You wave, too. Bare between us is the air. Fried bread for your lunch I make with a hole, give it to you behind the porch. In the chair, I don't sit all day, but leave that seat free to hold our hearts. I ain't got much to say you say, but will fill me with kisses, you will. To have everything I want, I say nothing. Quiet is where blessings are kept. All that the emptiness can hold is nothing anyone can steal. Every part of me no one ever sees or hears or holds, you keep. I am an empty jar.

Clea's Workday

She peels oranges. Skins limp as moths she sweeps out into tiny claws of grass that lean toward the back porch and grasp her scraps.

She pours tea and liquor. The house has its own brocade, it groans like pouring liquid, sound of thread quickly snapped. There is always laundry. The heft of wet sheets like a lover's weight. She mulches. Muddy roots bare their gullets. Upend the nettles.

She can play piano. But only turns music for the mistress to play. The sound of pages leafing is a dream of flight, oceans and wombs. Black flowers. Crushed seed. Spit on a hot iron.

She'll not run away, no more flesh for that.

Elbow bent to drive a hammer into nails. Weight of deciding where to make room for flower beds. Skulls from soil dug up, those souls curling out of bone. Drying fruit. Open windows.

Birds leave bare pines some wintertimes. An owl sometimes on a high branch. She lights a match, an everyday sound she loves.

She kindles the stove. Keeps broken cups. Ceramic, glass and zinc. She keeps cracked plates to decorate graves properly. There is always morning. For tending, there is always a thicket.

Zebedee Walking Behind Slave Quarters at Night

Some man is always smoking, tilting his head to watch stars.
A woman mouths *hush-hush* for a baby barely owned.
Sometimes fat is fried, a body is bent to fit a small grave.
What kind of life is this? A little bit of life, a broken branch
but not the whole tree. Someone sings a song, sounds like
she's singing, *You can't finish your life by living, your soul
don't need your body, just using it for a time.* When I dream
I am walking slowly, stepping on cracking twigs, thinking
I might just go ahead and die. What kind of life is this?
An old woman sewing at dawn bloomed
in shadows on the walls.
When she died, they made us break her like glass
to fit a round hole.
She sang, *What a spirit got to do with this skin, these bones?*
My little pain. There is this living. I don't know how
to let it go.

Zebedee Plans to Escape

Daytime pulls the dark over him. The snow hums silently silvering down. He sleeps like a felled tree, cut down from the others. Night jumbles dreams like a spilled box of nails. The wind is bullet smooth and quiet. He has a map in mind of paths through sudden hills. *Some bright morning when this life is o'er.* . . In the distance, a chalk-blue mountain rests against a smoky sky . . . *I'll fly away.*

To Auction

It's Monday in the morning and Zebedee the mulatto with his pools of blue as sky eyes is unsmiling with the others who run behind the carriage to keep warm and their feet and some bare feet sound mild upon the snow. Running and running to keep warm in the flurries. The master is taking Zebedee and them to be sold. The running is like our staying behind and is filled with the cold quiver of an animal just slit to its death, that last breath and its unblinking look before it dies. We ain't got much but half a heart amongst us anyway and just last night Zebedee telling me about box journeys. Says he's going to have himself packed up, shipped North with the mail and had a dream, he said, a dream. A dream that he was running far from this place along a river, thinking of taking me with him and he is running alright, and I have lost his hand and more. I watch them, and we watch them running far down in the snow for as long as we can not long before the morning bell rings to work it calls, and each ring is like a horse whip to break up my half piece of heart, like how skin will split in the cold.

Zebedee Is Sold and Caroline Works On

There is no window to watch. He is gone, I suppose. My view is the needle-tip, thin and silvery, poking up through ribbon and gown, glass beads I thread like silt across mistress' hem. I dream standing through the night to finish the dress. Shapeless sensations of brief salvation, a nod of sleep. *Please, Jesus, let that man stay outside of me.* The scent of bread from a kitchen I'm not allowed to enter. The scent of sweets I eat. On the back of my neck the mistress whips hard with switch made from a thin branch to wake me. In my mouth, like my baby suckling me, the taste of my own fingers—mineral and salty.

Tobias Finch Defends Selling Zebedee

On the platform, he looked like a fine horse or a plow. How could I? No part of me owns him now. Done I am with his shadow. Tobacco smoke. Fire. Give it time and Caroline will not recall. My wife is pleased. How can I be so cruel? You turn up your lip at me. My dog-bitten heart, my soul a sticky plate. He's no suckling. There's a man! Stood on the platform and they rubbed his tongue. Piano playing in the parlor. Quiet! He'll be fine. My Caroline. Bring me my cup of her flesh. Both breasts now mine.

Zebedee Tells What It's Like to Be Sold

When they tip my head back to look at my teeth
I see—

      the mouth of the iron bell
      wider, wider than an iron pot.
      Its tongue a black fist that makes music
      though its song is always the same.

That African Who Jumped Ship Jumps In with the Bad News about Zebedee

You want to think he got out. I tell you. . . Them old slaves were all too slow, too afraid to make a move. I just jump from the boat, die before all of this. But, these slaves always talkin', always flappin' their gums about running away. And why? Look at Clea and she. . . just some kitchen slave, just fodder for the old man to chew on. Look at what they did to her? But this mulatto? A blacksmith. Worth some silver, girl. You want to think of some good in all this. No good in it. That just your nowadays thinking, nonsense floating in the brain. Just like a shop full of those TVs you had, all showing nothing but snow.

Zebedee at the New Plantation

He resists me writing the word *new* in the title of this poem.
And the word *plantation* irritates him. He wants you to know
forge, anvil and hammer were the tools he had and never did he
touch a head of cotton. Tongs, vise and file carried in pockets
from the old Finch place to this place where he knew no one.
He would appreciate it if I did not make him sound lonely, he
wasn't. His idea, he wants you to know, was that God dwelled
in anything lacking language or tongue. Objects were right as
animals. He meant to name his tools in this way. Flame, heat
and smoke were his sisters. His being a slave was a certainty that
God existed for it made no other sense. He would like you to
know: his sledge weighed twelve pounds and anything heated
could be changed by its force. He doesn't want me to write
about his life anymore. He wants me to stop here. Don't tell of
how he spent the last of his lungs trying to run back home.

Thirteen Notes from Clea Unsent to Zebedee

One

Last night's sleep opened me to rooms furnished with strange eclipses and shards of broken julep glasses I buried out back.

Two

The waste of my tears cannot be estimated; time folds up each day in prayer.

Three

Backs have slices fit for angel's wings. Zeb, that you waving, body splintering into ash?

Four

Moonlight can't be traveled, escape triumphant only for dogs.

Five

There is a bell, a light and a bird in the air. Its wings are on fire to rush you away from that place.

Six

I chew wood and taste the plush of meat. My head holds the place we stood once, shared a stolen peach.

Seven

You hear the story about the tortoise and the rabbit, how he won the race? He had ten tortoise brothers all lined up along the way.

Eight

Snow turns to frost and then to a rain. Leaves build back on limbs.

Nine

My backmost tooth fell out all of a sudden last week! Thinking of you is like my tongue seeking that bloody place.

Ten

There is a turkey, a fly and the sun never going down. Come home before the moon rises high.

Eleven

I am dreaming they sell me, too, and bury my body like seed for grass. You come and lay yourself on the thousands of me greening tall enough to reach summer.

Twelve

A horse, an absence, a boy behind a plow. The earth unbraided, the sun revolves its wheels.

I see it from the kitchen where the devil comes in, seeking to devour me there.

Thirteen

At last I hear some news from you in sleep. Your ears echoing: *going high, going slow.* Open wide see teeth. Your silence hides a throat full of coins.

Escape with Shirt and Body

During the day when he walked, he outlined his hand in dirt again and again. One finger traced heat and curve of the other fingers, then changed hands, pressed palm into earth. Looked up, saw clouds and the frenzied shapes of leaves. Wiped his hands on his shirt. Each day, it was dirtier and dirtier, like the soiled fabric under the wounded on a bed. He wore it everyday forever, since being branded on his back. After that, he bled for three days and it left a stain—now rose-shaped and yellow as his skin. The color of sawdust, the shirt remembered his sweat, washed and re-sweated, like a cake soaked in syrup. It carried the memory of his mother who sewed it, dark hands needling it into shape; the sloped down-pull of the shoulders, now the wet armpits, collar smudged with grime. The shirt survived the journey, all the way to the last. Sopping with blood in front and under, to the exact place his body fell. Stuck to the motionless flesh that soon became a stench. The inevitable revelation of bones that in the heat unravel certainly, deftly as his mother had first uncoiled thread, and the shirt—on his back—was slowly absorbed into the earth.

Clea Gives Up Waiting

I look for omens. To leave or be taken, I hope. I wouldn't mind being dead. Some mornings the sky is so hungry white I am sure it is the end. Yolk-yellow sun moving, make me blind. Raisins in the batter, wet dough in boiling oil. Dark as eyelashes are my thoughts. Dead I'll be. I drop julep glasses; they glitter on the thrice-washed floor. To bury them in the garden I go. Bad sign. Only the living heart clings to fear. To die, I am willing. Three white owls last night. Some chickens gone missing. That rapture I envy. The mistress comes counting, looks for my breaking. Springtime bluebells will burst up bluer from where they grew with glass.

Prudence Finch's Dream about Clea

You appeared at the piano in the parlor your last day. I said, You are free.

Your voice still rings like the church bell. Hands gestured sentences. You spooled words tight and kept the spiral inside. I always knew what you didn't say would blacken our flesh to ashes.

Languishing in his empty room, my father struck the dinner bell, the breakfast bell, the call for cigars and bourbon. You came on cue. He isn't anymore, not even in my dreams.

We are figures in paintings. My eyes painted this way, yours painted like that. Let me smell your hair again, its grassy and nutty hue.

In my dream, you looked out the window. You wanted it open. The beams you wanted removed, the roof burned to its edges. You needed to fly out. Leaving through the back door wouldn't do.

Better to remember things proper. You are gone long as years on more hands counted than two. I am still a branch on my father's tree. Kind I was, but I never did leave the corners of his house.

This dream of you is better memory than remembering you going. Go on, Clea. Fly out in your black crow dress.

The Last Days of Slavery

There was talk they'd free all slaves. I kept none but my Caroline. Oh, heart in a fist, you could fry it in oil and swallow it with whiskey. My wife would not cook for me. Cold food. I sold as many as I could: babies went slow; for the boys, I got my can of coins. Caroline, I would not let go. Oh, blood draining in a bowl kept time like a run-down clock. They all left my house, my fields drowned in dust. Caroline, her mouth tight as a rosebud; my fingers knew her stem.

Caroline's Side of the Story

The day the others got freedom, I stayed. Master said he'd pay me handsome and then I could too be free, but have a crown, hair plaited like a queen. I'm a fool, you say. The mind is full of empty rooms with spiders and wheels, I say. Nowhere to go that there was not nowhere to be. I wear all the dresses I made for the mistress now. To her funeral, the white muslin with a soft, fur yoke. Master too old to finger me after a time. That man bought me for a handful of coins to live my small life in his mouth. Poor girl, you say? I tell you, eternity is long and even Judas still rots in his potter's grave.

Clea, Circa 1905

My house this is. None of those clocks and lamps, but a good stove I got. Piano's mine. The only use-to-be-slave around here got a piano. Don't play it often. An old sound it has, old as them times with orange rind jammed under my nails, peeling for ices. I ate so many that one day because old Finch was at auction and never to count did the missus bother. Was good, them oranges. A little something sweet there always is. The day I filled my mouth with oranges was the same day they took my sweetheart to be sold. Some salty tears I cried that day. Oranges and salt. Hominy and cheese for supper. Oil in lamps, but only inside me, my body all lit up like noon. No more hours now. No more light. My beloved is a crow hopping on one foot.

Plenty

From the plantation walking to nowhere the day we
    were freed.
        One hand over our faces to hide the sun.
                         Dry wind in dry grass.
Blind man's cane switching from side to side.
Singing, someone was: *Do Lord, O do Lord, do remember me.*
                 We were going to the river.
We had no thoughts,
    filed our edges and prayed for plenty.

I paused in the dull shade of every being burned in me.
    Pots and pans I carried on my back, the kitchen come
        with me.
    Prayed, I did: Beloved God, the fish we caught today!
Make them multiply.
Old man made a fire, I fried them up in a pan.
    Fish—another word for miracle.
Water perfect around them, the way my body keeps my soul.

        Trout: when I eat you, I am every inch a river.

iii.

The Slaves Arrive and Do Not Leave for Months

I take dictation from the slaves for three weeks and then begin to bring home flowers. My apartment becomes their grave. A roomy casket they are impressed with, glad that death has turned out so good. They lie down in pairs and discuss life back then as I sleep. They lick newspapers for words. They chew up books like bad dogs. And so, my dreams are noisy with their nonsense, their ugly tales. A teacher says that I cannot be the narrator of their story, I've got to get one of them to do it. Clea? Caroline? Maybe Zebedee. I try for a year and that is when they disappear. Or rather, they fade and droop, their heads like sweet old lilies. Their stems gone soggy in all that water.

Clea's Ghost Comes for an Extended Visit

Clea does not respond to the other slaves' stories and she is undaunted by Zebedee's presence in the room. To say she ignores him is to say she might be deaf. Or, she might just not care anymore. She goes about my place making dust behind the counters, letting in flies and turning the cheese to mold. She also makes orchids bloom and creates a nice echo in the bathroom, where I can sing. She's always wearing that black crow dress.

Zebedee States the Reason for His Visit

I am jealous of your funerals. Of the men wearing hats and women in dark stockings. My longings accumulate. Death is strict and sharp. Birds molt feathers, trees shed leaves and the earth takes them in. I am jealous of your funerals. I love the singing, the vibrato shimmering in the church like schools of fish swimming. I want to carry a suitcase again. Let me drink some punch; I don't recall the flavor. There is consolation in the folding of metal chairs. The autumnal talk at the house afterwards, the way mourners tell quiet jokes then feel the uneasy timidity of being alive. No slave ever got a sending off. I sleep without a marker. Think of me. Like a stone, leave me for ages under a cypress then carry me for a while in your pocket, throw me into another river. No more. I am jealous of your funerals. I watch the past for long stretches. Come here, I will show you something of forgetting. How even a bleeding thumb announces its heartbeat. I want the feeling of being buried.

Dream Visitor

Voice hovering like moonlight on a pond, the fugitive arrives when I turn the lamp out. He agitates like a siren or a pounding rain. An ancestor the color of cedar, his breath bluesy from drinking whiskey. I won't kiss his cheek but I can't turn away. Our eyes shut like the dead, we soft-shoe in the kitchen's bright air to music lodged in his one good ear. In dreams, he hollers as feet twitch under clean white sheets where muscles remember running is how to get free. There was no chance to sleep then, just lying under a house waiting for bounty hunters to leave. This morning, he played piano and I thought he'd sing, but his mouth held tight to the shape *Oh!* like the mouth of his cold body on a weedy back road.

Clea, Living and Dying

Been born five times, four times black. Progress of me unsteady as a sparrow branch-gripped in wind.

That slave time, I don't want to hear no tell. Of chains and sea trips. My missing finger. Longed for comfort to come like Jesus in the cool of the day, but there always was locusts.

My eye got shot in a war. A glass one I had, plopped it in an old jam jar that watched me when I woke.

Pretenses I had. One life spoke Creole. Wore a whiskery white suit.

Once, a saint; my soul clung to God the way an egg grips its separate parts.

Born white one time. With hands full of mathematics. My lover was numbers. Can't say any of the bodies I had for hundreds of years was finer.

Each life walks parallel streets at the same pace. I am dead in each. Time is the devil, but I ain't saying he's fast. All my rooms are quiet like the dark after fire.

All things go on past. Jesus be with me to the end. To die and live outside my mind without a mirror. Show me roots below the hours. The heart in its jerky box. Driving rain holds the answer. I think I'll go on and be glad.

Gather up my thoughts, scatter like wasps. In my hand, a broken bowl.

The Slaves Remember the End

Piled snow and the moon at 3 o'clock. Jars empty, jars full.
Massa sits in a chair with a rifle on his knees. All of us slaves
gone last year. Not a penny for our sacks. His heart always was a
dull knife. His chest full of hiccups and a bottle of rye. He loved
his Caroline. He must hear she loves him or out she'll stay with
the snow and moon. Moon and snow. She keeps her mouth dry
as a closed book. He'll bury her right, a hole through the head
when she's too cold to know. Then, a mouthful of rifle for his
own. Piled snow and a moon high in the night.

Caroline Confronts Tobias Finch

He let me die in the snow. If I ever forgive him, we can both have our rest. But, as long as there are shadows, I suppose I'll stay. I wish he would not sigh so loud. We both haunt that place, equal at last. He say, *We're souls now, just the dried pit of eaten fruit. Let me go, Caroline, let me go.* He say, *Our minds and bodies did things without consulting our souls.* I think of his body now, its ashes heaped in a box. Mine scattered for birds where he let me die in the snow. I still taste that cold. He say, *I'd be sorry but it wasn't* me *who did that, but the mind that held me captive.* My trespasser, you fed me from your tongue. You let me live. You let me die in the snow. This garden is mine. Some winters, I eat the crocus bulbs. Some summers, I green the grass. What a revelation! You follow *me* now, hollering through every season, saying, *Caroline, let me go.*

What Clea Says Before She Goes

What kind of past is this?   Each morning after yesterday,
  I go to the valley of bones.

The only color is the color of skulls.   Still as hawks.
     The sun gloats.

God's infrequent breath is windy.   I ask you, was
there a

  fig you tasted once?
                      A slice of cake?

It's not trivial living a life.   There is so many of us now.
       Whoever you are, help me search through these
skins.

Boxes of hearts.   Two belong to me.

     I ask you, what kind of heaven is this?
Our   bodies   mere
seeds.   We bloomed to our deaths like smoke
  or new branches.

The husks I love.   My mouth is dry.

Every evening after this life is a resurrection.
    The stones cry out.

Slaves Out Back in My Garden Among the Zinnias Are

singing—*Death is a simple thing, he go from door to door.* Say—this here's how we stay alive: we pocket stones. Our favorite scripture is, *Jesus wept* and so we got to feel no shame. This is our hammer— we use the forked end to pull nails from our hopes. This here's how a mother let go a child to be sold. Here's how we beat out birds to hide in trees. Afraid we were, but knew even Jesus had no bed. Zinnias all over the place! Where's your rock garden, girl? We need something stronger to keep the dust around our roots from going. Enough time here we've had, though. Here's two stories we love to tell: Jesus slept on a boat during a storm; Pharaoh's army drowned. *Death is a simple thing, he go from door to door.* Sometimes, we tremble.

Goodbye to My Favorite Ghost, Clea

Clea, ghost tentative as a memorized poem, you're leaving me. The pipes will go silent after all your knocking. My records will stop skipping. Your one milky-glass eye that thrilled me with its magnifications, its ability to divide all you saw into infinite variations, will close. Hold off silence until the last minute, turn up the volume as the music fades out. Keep ringing your leaving in the breeze—bell chime, flighty mosquito, crow. Take this tool: unhinge every single plantation door on your way out— hum a loose, winterly tune. Now, put your hands in the loam, pull damp moss from the earth's scalp—a pillow for your grave. You old slave, genius, soldier, ghost. However many lives you live, the first one is always the worst. Church bells are ringing: *ring ring ring*. . . That's you, Clea, you keep on singing: *On home to dust my body goes.*

Recent Titles from Alice James Books

Alice James Books has been publishing poetry since 1973 and remains one of the few presses in the country that is run collectively. The cooperative selects manuscripts for publication primarily through regional and national annual competitions. Authors who win a Kinereth Gensler Award become active members of the cooperative board and participate in the editorial decisions of the press. The press, which historically has placed an emphasis on publishing women poets, was named for Alice James, sister of William and Henry, whose fine journal and gift for writing went unrecognized during her lifetime.

Typeset and Designed by
Pamela A. Consolazio

Printed by Thomson-Shore
on 30% postconsumer recycled paper
processed chlorine-free